1975

University of St. Francis
GEN 811.5 L316g
Larsen
Godsee'

S0-ACL-800

book may be

'N DAYS

GODSEEKERS

1975

GODSEEKERS

EARNEST LARSEN

LIBRARY
College of St. Francis
JOLIET, ILL.

AVE MARIA PRESS
Notre Dame, Indiana 46556

Library of Congress Catalog Card Number: 74-26323

International Standard Book Number: 0-87793-088-0

© 1975 Ave Maria Press, Notre Dame, IN 46556
All rights reserved

Photography: pages 4, 5, 6, 8, 68, 92 and 111, *Kitty Schmitt*
             page 44, *Eddy Tribble*

Printed in the United States of America

811.5
L316g

To the seekers I love
fighting their way through
the long night's fog into
brilliant light.

71876

Contents

QUESTION 1
Whom Do You Seek?

THE WORLD has much of beauty,
peace and hope.
But the street is also full
of heartache.
Pain, even if hidden and secret, abounds.
Behind the walls of many smiles
sits its owner in tears.

People are madly running—
some toward something, searching,
some just running away.
Some aren't sure which, only that
they must run.

Pressure becomes too great.
Pressure to live up to expectations,
to communicate,
to make ends meet,
to get along with everyone else,
when often
we can't even get along with ourselves.
On the one hand we try to
keep things simple,
on the other we hate to be or do
things alone.

Yet
as soon as others are involved
in our plans, things get so complicated.
Mostly everything done with others—
even such a simple operation as a picnic—
gets to be such a hassle; so much
pushing and shoving.
It's easier alone,
so it seems.

Often it appears predestined by God
that the only things I really want
are those
I cannot lay my hands on.
And that torments me.
Where is God?
If he can and does work,
why doesn't he?

"God doesn't work"
is the complaint of many heartsick believers.
In all honesty, what they often
feel toward God
is that they have been cheated and let down.
Or that he is hidden so well
they just can't find him.
Maybe that's the problem.

Having started this way, I suppose the
expectation is that
now I tell you why he does work
and how to find him.
The first lines of this meditation seem
a perfect, contrived setup.
Construct a problem, then
come riding down with some surefire reasoning
that mothers, spouses, ministers can spring
on those who experience finding God difficult
and make them content in their faith.

There is no surefire way.
There is no technique that
guarantees the results we are sure
coincide with the timetable and results
God wants.
What there can be, however,
which may be of great help, is
to consider the right questions.
In the light of all the heartbreak,
all the running and seeking,
we ask questions all right.
But are they the right ones?
There are no right answers to
wrong questions
and when it comes to God, mostly
we have forgotten the questions.

We have great answers but
what are the questions?
To lose sight of the question
is to lose sight of our direction.
And when this happens,
all that is left is
idol worship.
Perhaps that is what many Christians have
     today,
both those who seek and those who think
they have found—an idol.
Perhaps that is what many who are
just running
are running from,
an idol named God.

Three genuine questions we might consider
before we start worrying about
design of our church buildings,
the texture of our hosts and
the size of our banners are:
    1) Who is God, this God we claim we seek?
    2) What do we ask of God?
    3) How do we seek?
Without the insight and direction that
comes from serious consideration of these
      questions,
the streets remain flowing with tears,
the lost remain in confusion
and those who would offer light find
their candles have gone out.

The right questions are essential because
seeking and finding are
two different things entirely.
It is true that only those who seek
can find—but seeking
doesn't necessarily mean you will find.
It depends on where and how you seek,
it depends on your desperation
from which comes determination
in the search.
You can seek all the serenity you want
by getting more things, yet
you will always hunger for more;
you can seek all the love you want by
possessing those
whom you would be loved by and
yet you will never break love's bread;
you can seek strength
by never admitting you have a weakness

or acknowledging your needs and
your strength will be your weakness.
Seeking does not mean finding.
Finding means successful seeking.
And that requires asking the correct questions.
Right questions are like
right keys
in trying to open a lock.
In seeking God we so often don't use
the right keys.

"Why doesn't God help me?"
said Don. He was serious.
"I've done all I can for him,
contributed to the Church, said prayers,
gone to Mass often—
all I want is financial security.
I want to be as class as my neighbor,
and it doesn't happen.
I'm not wealthy or secure.
God doesn't work."

Is that the question?

Bill had a different question.
Like the rest of us, he has a major
character defect. His own special demon.
There is nothing (almost) he wouldn't do
to get it under control.
Control is God's business, isn't it?
So he shot some of his best prayers
at God.
He offered to make a deal:
"Get me over this problem
and I will never mess around again."
That sounds like a deal
God
should be interested in.
But the problem continued,

he still is plagued by his
character defect.
He wanted instant curing and
was willing to "pay" for it.
But God apparently didn't have the
power to take care of the deal.
So, see, God doesn't work.

Is that the question?

Cathy is altogether different,
kind of. She is on the road now.
Cathy, like hundreds of thousands of her
brothers and sisters, is looking to
"find her head."
What does it mean to live,
what do I want to do,
where is "it" at?
She was raised a churchgoer
and has gone all her life.
But she is so restless and
God doesn't seem to help.
"If he is so great, why doesn't he
answer my questions?" she says.
That was some time ago though.
She stopped asking that question;
God (as she understands him) is just no longer
important.
He has been tried and found wanting.
I itched and he didn't scratch me.

Is that the question?

15 / WHOM DO YOU SEEK?

To find is to seek successfully, which
means seeking what can be found.
What these people seek,
and so many others, is
not God.
They are seeking an idol
which they call God.
But the problem with idols
is that they have no power,
neither in themselves or to
effect change in their worshipers.
Idols don't work.
God does.
And as the prayer goes,
". . . God, grant me the wisdom to
know the difference."
Don, Bill and Cathy sought God
(or something)
by setting their conditions and trying
to negotiate a deal.
At one time they were sure
"God is the answer," but
to what question?

There are also those who find themselves or
their loved ones sick
and demand God heal them;
those who are depressed and pray,
yet they remain depressed.
There are those struck down by some
disaster
who find they cannot forgive God;
those wounded by all the
"changes in religion"
who somehow lost God in the shuffle.

And there are those who don't even know
their God is an idol,
those who have not been shaken to the point
where they ask new questions and
seek new light.
These are too comfortable.
God, for them, is security.
Everything is fine.
God is their boat
so let the storm come;
they
are taken care of.
Who knows or cares about anyone else?
THEY
are safe.

Father Andrew Greeley, in his book
The Sinai Myth,
quotes a sociological survey which revealed
that the most bigoted people in America
were also the most externally religious.
They were the ones whose prayers and
words
justified their "rightness" in keeping
others down "in their place."
It's the old story of
"God's on our side," and
therefore, obviously, he isn't on
"their" side.
Therefore, we are free to
kill, cruelly gossip about and persecute
"them";
it will be a favor to God.
Having placed themselves in his judgment seat,
they can then wage "religious wars."

Perhaps we are not too far out of line
to suggest
that many of our churches may be filled
with idol worshipers reciting
the Lord's prayer every week
while brothers and sisters suffer
in isolation at our elbow
without our trying to free them
or ourselves
from the slavery we are not even aware of.

Perhaps the appropriate question
is not, "Why doesn't God play my game?"
        but
"Am I playing his game?"
But
what is God's game,
the only game he deals in?
And who is this God?
What is this God
we are so sure we know so much about,
yet have such difficulty touching?

It just might be that, if
we deal with these real questions,
we will find we don't
want to find God.
Perhaps we will hear him asking something
far different than what
we are prepared to give.

GOD WHO?

In considering this essential question,
"God who?"
there is an obvious (or not so obvious)
trap to be avoided.
Contemplating the "who-ness" of God
can be a head trip leading nowhere.

We cannot know who God is.
Gregory Nazianzen, an ancient Father of the
    Church,
was talking about just this ego trip when
he said of an Arian spokesman
(Arianism was a heresy of the early centuries):
". . . he speaks on the generation of the Son
as if
he had been there as midwife."
The great Thomas Aquinas
says the same thing from
a different standpoint:
". . . one thing about God remains
completely unknown in this life,
namely,
what God is."
Also the important contemporary theologian,
    the late
John Courtney Murray, in commenting on
the teachings of Thomas, wisely states that
"Aquinas' analogy of being . . . lets us know
    that,
when we are thinking or talking about God,
it is really about God we are thinking and
    talking.
It does not assure us that
WHAT
we think and say about God
IS
what God is."

We can know that God is;
we cannot know what God is.
Murray states that ignorance
after exhaustive investigation
is the only possible result of this
question.
Ignorance not meaning stupidity
but lack of knowledge.
Not that nothing can be known
but that full understanding,
total grasping,
mind-engulfing comprehension
is impossible.
But something can be known,
and that is,
God loves us.

How utterly simplistic!
How trite beyond words to tell!
In the face of the world's misery
and incompleteness,
it seems almost an insult to
recite such a
sugar-coated platitude.
Any third-grader knows
that God loves him.
True,
but how great the chasm between knowing
and accepting.
And perhaps the real tragedy is how few
there are who can accept that
God or anyone else loves them.

Maybe underneath much of the
heartbreak around us is
this very fact:
the inability to love or
be loved—
the lies we conjure up to
hide this fact and
the poison fruit we eat
trying to substitute for it.

Finding involves asking the
right questions.
Do you, can you
accept that God loves you?
Can you, for that matter,
accept that anyone loves you?

Rather than face and deal with this
real question,
many people would prefer to construct and
        then worship an
idol named God.

Loving,
both in giving and accepting,
is no small matter.
It is not easy.
Most of us fear it beyond
all else.
We name the problem something else,
        of course—
something like
I don't want to be involved,
no one cares,
I'm not worthy of it,
love is weakness.
But there, at the bottom of it all,

are the art and freedom of loving
never developed.
And for all that we don't know
of what God is,
there is this that faith proclaims:
"God loves you."
For all the infinite unknowableness
of the Divine,
there is this Covenant fact,
for some reason making sense only to God:
He has chosen you,
He has called you by name,
He has claimed you for his own
and
He loves you.
Either find God along that road
or idols are all that is left.

All psychologists, sociologists,
even anthropologists worthy of their names
can tell us why contemporary men find it
difficult to love.
They tell us of the "uprootedness"
of modern society,
the alienation and need for community.
There are reasons,
valid and all too tragic reasons,
which don't change the fact that it is so.
Yet it is precisely along this
most difficult road
that the God of history proclaims his name
among men.
The question of "God who?"
is intimately twined with the question,
"Can you, will you accept love?"
On any other level,
no,
God doesn't work
because it isn't God.
Finding God always means growing
to the point of accepting love.

INAUTHENTIC LOVE

The more precious any "real McCoy,"
the more fakes abound.
There is much inauthentic love.
Much that passes for love
(and God)
that is hollow at its core.
And this not only by conscious deception
(if you love me, cheat for me, lie for me,
let me do what I want—which of course cannot
ever be love),
but also from a far deeper level.
We most often are not deliberate idol-
     worshipers,
it is just that real loving is so difficult
and it is so easy to place a substitute on the
altar of the living God.

Authentic love trusts,
inauthentic love does not.
How countlessly many times we would
say something, do something, write something
to one we love
BUT
we fear they would not accept it,
they would think it silly,
they would not understand.
In effect,
we don't trust enough.
It may well be they *would*
accept and understand;
that isn't the problem.

The problem is we don't trust them enough
to give the gift of our trust.
We can give a loved one gifts
and die a thousand deaths over the worry,
"Will it be good enough?"
The question,
"Would it be good enough for you
if the situation were reversed?"
seems silly.
"Of course! That's different."
Is it?
Why?
Because one is you giving and
the other is you receiving.

Often we don't have great trouble giving our
compassion, concern, money or time—
but we do receiving.
To be on the receiving end of a love-gift
is pain beyond our power to bear.
We are such strangers to the wisdom that
receiving is the greatest giving.

Authentic love not only forgives
(which is a form of giving)
but accepts that they are forgiven.
To accept forgiveness means
you don't go around flogging yourself
for a mistake or failure,
because to be loved is to accept
that you don't have to carry around the facade,
the mask
of perfection.

In love the sense of needing forgiveness
first of all arises
not because a law was broken but
because a relationship was dishonored.
Laws are not relationships.
There is all the difference in the world
between the situation of
"I'm sorry I was late, I know
we eat at six"
and
"I'm sorry I'm late, I know
how important it is that we are all together
for bread-breaking."

God who?
Can we accept that it is
I-LOVE-YOU
speaking to us in and through
his Son Jesus, acting in us
through the Spirit who is love?
It's either that or
an idol.

Is it so trite to merely say,
"God loves you"?
Then why such huge cargoes of guilt
carried all around us,
why so many statements like
"God might be God but he can't forgive
me,
I am too big a sinner."
And even more the sister thoughts,
"Sure God is a God of love;
he loves my mother and dad,
my husband, wife, kids and
neighbors—
he loves the bishops and the pope,
the organist and the religious coordinator,
but not me.
You see,
I don't think I'm worthy of being loved."
Enter idols.

25 / WHOM DO YOU SEEK?

Yes, you are worthy of being loved.
Even you.
And God does.
There is no other way
to see his face than
to surrender to this basic, fundamental, intimate
Covenant truth:
God loves you.

We all know from our sources of
pop psychology:
records, books, soap operas, TV programs,
that you can't buy love.
All the money in the world can't do it;
nor can you possess a loved one.
You can possess things, not people.
You can't love what you possess;
you only love what you desire to set free.

Any attempt to manipulate love
by its very nature
diminishes that love.
Gifts to a loved one
are not for manipulation
(if it is love)
but are merely an expression that
love is.
The mode of expression becomes not
the central issue
but the fact that there is something
to express.
Love does not try to buy or force
the beloved
into playing your game
but frees him to
play his own best game.

71876

LIBRARY
College of St. Francis
JOLIET, ILL.

All the "I give you this if
you will give me that" talk
is not in the vocabulary of love.
Rather, "I give you this freely,
no strings attached,
because you are precious to me,
because I love you,
because I want you to know you
are loved."
Anything else is not love.

"God doesn't work!
I prayed and nothing happened!"
God who?

Waltzing through my mind
are many faces, mostly of young people,
who say,
"It can't be. There is no
love like that.
There is no giving with
no strings attached;
no one does anything just to say,
'You are precious to me.' "
And thus they
have named their problem with God.
Because God does.

As unscientific, as simplistic theologically
as this sounds—it is a faith-truth;
this is precisely how and why God loves you:
freely,
because you are precious and he
has chosen to do so.

The old tapes
start whirling frantically:
I'm not worth it,
I can't swallow that,
it's too hard,
there is too much responsibility . . .
but at least they are related
to the right question.
All of these are valid reasons for
rejecting God—
accepting love is agonizingly difficult.
It demands a surrender.
If God is rejected on these terms,
at least it is God who has been rejected
and not some silly, hideous idol.

How often this happens!
God is reduced to an idol,
the idol is rejected as unacceptable,
rightly so for any thinking, serious faith-seeker,
but the idol is still called God,
not idol.
It were as if what was believed in was God.
Rejecting idols is the first step toward finding
        God.
Idols cannot answer real questions,
but only real questions pave the way
to the Real who is God;
real questions
such as those concerning
accepting love.

MYTHOLOGY

Besides our plain psychological lack of
      freedom
in accepting love
(which, as we have seen, has great bearing on
why we sometimes say God doesn't work),
there is the difficulty of what
Father Eugene Kennedy, among others, calls
bad mythology.
Myths are not fairy tales.
Myths are the meaning systems we assign
realities in our lives.
According to the way we understand our myths
we treat these realities.
If our myth of America is
"my country right or wrong" and
"God is on our side," meaning
to the exclusion of everyone else,
then that is how we will treat America.
That is how we understand its meaning.
But if our "myth of America" is that
it is a country made of people,
which means it will be imperfect;
that together we will work to make what is
      right
better
and what is wrong
we will eradicate, then
we will treat America in that manner.
For that is our myth.

There are those whose myth of
welfare is that everyone on welfare
is a liar and a cheat;
that all whites are cruel and greedy;
that all suburbs are without problems;
that any man who exhibits sensitivity is
no man at all.
We live out our whole lives within and
acting out the myths
which we inherited or constructed
about the world all around us.
There are myths telling us what
men and women are
and are supposed to be,
There are myths interpreting the meaning of
being wealthy or poor
(like, no one wealthy is ever happy and
no one poor is ever sad).
All nationalities and races are
veiled in myth,
as are all religions.

Even such a prosaic thing as
the "Wild West" is myth.
Luther Standing Bear, born in 1868, was a chief
of the Oglala band of Sioux.
He tells us of the
"old way" of the Indian:
"We did not think of the great open plains,
the beautiful rolling hills
and the winding streams with tangled growth
as 'wild.'

Only to the white man was nature
a wilderness and only to him was the land
'infested' with 'wild animals' and 'savages.'
To us it was tame.
Earth was bountiful and
we were surrounded with the blessings of
The Great Mystery.
Not until the hairy man from the east
came and with brutal frenzy heaped
injustices upon us and the families we loved
was it 'wild' for us.
When the very animals of the forest began
fleeing his approach,
then it was that
for us
the 'Wild West' began."

It is a matter of mythology,
of meaning systems, of how we
view and understand any reality,
that makes them, for us,
to be what they are.
Even with the "Wild West."
And there is our God myth.

As with all myths,
our myth of God
can be either good or bad,
true or false,
based on honesty or dishonesty.
"God who?" is no idle question.
It is a question about our understanding this
being, this Person
we call God.
It is an essential question.

Jesus often questioned his apostles on
their mythology of God who was present
    among them
in the form of himself.
"Who do the crowds say that I am?" he asked.
In other words,
what is your God-mythology?
The apostles responded with several
erroneous concepts:
"Some say you are John the Baptizer, or
Elijah or one of the old prophets returned
from the dead."
But then Jesus asked the vital question,
vital to our whole consideration of
the idol named God:
"But you," he said, "who do you say that I
    am?"
God who?
A bad (false) mythology spells
I-D-O-L.
And idols don't work.

In place of accepting love
it is very possible to reduce God to law
and make of law a god.
Not that law is bad,
it is only bad when we put the face of
God on it.
Father Greeley,
again in his book, *The Sinai Myth,*
has a striking section on the immense efforts
many churchgoers expend to please God by
going to church, saying novena prayers,
    reciting rosaries,
abstaining from certain food at certain times,
    etc.,
and then he says we find out
God doesn't care one little bit if we do them
    all
or not.

At first sight it might sound
blasphemous to say such a thing.
Imagine,
after all this time and the thousands of
sermons, warnings and lectures on
You had better go to Mass,
and now to say God doesn't care one way
 or another.
But that was not his point.
The point is, when obeying the law
about churchgoing becomes the center of
religion,
then we no longer have religion.
Religion (as Christians understand it)
is accepting that God loves us.

Placing an ethical system
at the center of Christianity is so
much a part of our heritage that we scarcely
are aware what a subtle idol it can become.
Rectory offices around the country
are flooded with calls every
"holy day of obligation"
about if it is still a sin to miss Mass;
on Fridays during Lent, if it is a sin
to eat meat;
if it is a sin to miss church while on
summer vacation;
if it is a sin to see this movie
or read that book.
Obsession with sin
has driven many people from the Church.
But sin is not the core of
Christ's way for man,
accepting his love is
his way.
What does not come from that core
leads to a false temple.

This, of course, is not to say
that there is no sin
or that it matters not at all whether we
sin or not.
Of course there is sin
and of course it matters if we are
guilty of love-breaking.
The point is, we cannot
"lose our sense of sin,"
as Pius XII lamented decades ago,
without first of all losing our
sense of personal love for and
from God.

If a poll were taken of Christians
(which includes Catholics)
as to what they considered the indispensable
core of Christianity to be,
I'd wager they would respond in majority,
"If you die with sin on your soul,
you will go to hell;
if you die not in mortal sin, you
will go to heaven."
Such was not the basic message of
the Covenant of Sinai to Moses;
it was not the core message of Easter;
it most certainly was not the prime proclama-
    tion of
Pentecost.
The truth of these religious events was,
"God has loved you; you are his;
with Christ you have passed from
death to life."
Jesus could not have put it more plainly:
"I have come that you may have life
and have it more abundantly."
". . . and who do you
say that I am?"

The myth of the cosmic problem-solver
is also deeply ingrained in us.
We have been told that God is
omnipotent, which means he can do anything.
We are also told he cares for us.
Therefore, it stands to reason if he *can* do
    everything
and if he cares for me,
then let him do his stuff.
We offer a great many sincere,
heartfelt prayers
to the problem-solver in the sky.
When the problem does improve,
we say, "See, God took care of it."
When the problem gets worse, we say,
"God doesn't work," or
"He's slow but he'll make it come out right
    some way."

But again we must return to our
original premise:
only authentic seeking will yield
genuine finding.
Authentic seeking requires
asking the right questions.
Is this what God declared himself
to be — problem-solver —
through his Son Jesus Christ?
Of course God is
omnipotent
but he is not some version of the
strong man in a circus;
He is not "here" to
"walk across our swimming pool."
And the whole point of revelation is
that he does care,
passionately,
about his people.
But is solving our problems God's game?

Perhaps we are not even aware of
what kind of problems
God deals with.
Following Pentecost the apostles
had lots of "problems."
People were trying to kill them.
That is quite a problem.
They were confused by much in their culture
as it related to their task.
Another problem.
At times they couldn't even get along with
one another.
Now if God were a problem-solver,
surely he would solve their problems,
if anyone's.
Solve them in the way
we think
he should go about it.
He did not.
One by one they were tracked down
and murdered.
The doubt over dissension remained.
Problems multiplied.
Yet the post-Pentecost apostles
did not shout,
"God doesn't work!"

No, they were dealing with other
matters than things going smoothly
or retaining their personal health.

So with Jesus.
What problems he had!
No one understood what he was trying to say.
People were using him fearfully.
He was lonely and discouraged.
His life was running a path that could only end
in destruction.

Surely,
if God works,
he would solve Jesus' problems
in some painless fashion.
But did he?
Jesus was murdered,
the proto-victim of all to come.
He died alone and mocked.

This presents a stark contrast
to our concept,
our mythology,
of what God ought to be.
According to our questions
his answers don't make sense;
not then, often not now.
We keep asking the same questions
about laws and travelers' aid
and keep getting these strange answers.
Especially
when we hold our demands up against the
"problems" of Christ and the apostles.

What is our mythology of God?
Is it genuinely God we seek,
or is it rather a super Valium pill
to make the tensions of the world disappear?
And if it is an idol we truly seek,
then we have no complaint when we receive
        an
idol's response.

The final bad mythology we shall touch on
is the myth of doing.
It is not merely a bad God myth;
it is also a bad American myth.
This meaning system tells us that
doing is good.
Action produces and production is what
progress is all about.
So get busy and do something.
As this relates to God
it tells us that God can be made happy
by a great amount of activity.
At the center of revelation
is not an all-loving God
achingly inviting us to love in return
but
a computer keeping count of all our
good works.

Again,
the point is not that good works
are not important; they are.
The point is that
the good works,
just like observance of the laws,
must come from a core of
reciprocal love.
That is what gives them meaning and
genuine power.

God does not love us
because
we do good things.
He loves us just because he does.
He does not love us only when
we avoid sin;
He loves us even as sinners.
He loves us.
All of us.
All of the time.
Perhaps he does not love everything we do;
He does not love the slavery that we
retain in the face of his offered freedom,
but he loves us.

There is a lack of serenity,
a lack of relaxed peace,
at the center of a person who has replaced
do-ism for God.
Such people are compelled
out of a bad mythology to increase
production of good works
in order to please God.
It is much like a salesman who
must continually sell more this year
than last.
His production becomes his own point of
    competition
and also the source of his
nervous breakdown.
We are not in competition with anyone else
over God's love.
We are not even in competition
with ourselves over good works done
to "win" God's approval.

Is such the case with anyone you love
or who loves you?
Must you win someone else's love,
prove it continually to them
lest they forget or not trust your commitment?
Such an attitude betrays a juvenile concept of
love, to be sure.
And God asks for juvenile love only
from juveniles.

Obeying laws,
saying prayers,
doing good works are all necessary;
but
they are also a matter of our doing.
Our doing is not what makes God work.
Only God makes God work.
The only thing we *have* to do in seeking
and finding God
is to surrender.

SURRENDER

Surrender is not compliance.
Compliance is merely an outward expression
of what might well not be inner at all.
God does not ask us to comply
to laws, rituals and words;
he asks us to accept his love and
thus love in return.
Surrendering to the infinite God is a
surrender to love;
it is the same paradox St. Paul speaks of when
      he says,
"It is only in infirmity that I am
made strong."
Only when I lay my infirmity down,
admitting it,
asking for help with it,
dealing with it,
that I can lay claim to the power of God.

Surrender does not mean I give up,
that I stop trying.
Faith-surrender means I stop
trying to do it all alone.
It means I acknowledge that abundant, free life
is God's game,
that man coming to full life is his
holy will;
that my freedom is his wish for me.
No person can accomplish this understanding
      of
God's will
by himself.
The real question is, will I
let go and let God?
For if I won't let God, then my only remaining
option is to attempt to
be God.
Which is an idol.

In all of our lives there is a point
beyond which we cannot go.
Not by ourselves.
There is a resentment that must be
given up,
an addiction that must yield to freedom,
a death that must be coped with —
something.
Up until that point we seem to
manage things pretty well by ourselves.
Up until then we may say,
"God, I need you,"
but like the apostles in the boat before the
    storm,
we don't know if we really believe that or not.
We've never been tested.
Then the storm.
Then the waves and fearful lightning.
Then the calling out to God —
and if it is truly God and
if we are asking the right questions,
for many it is the first time in a possibly long
religious life
that God is ever met.
As one man said,
"The best place to find God is
kissing concrete."
What the "concrete" is in our lives will vary,
but not the coming to the point beyond which
only God's liberating power can take us.
Not because he has to,
not because we have earned it —
but because he loves us.
Freely.
Just because he does.
Is that our God?
Is that your God?

Let us suggest this idol-tester:
We are all familiar with St. Paul's definition
of love to the Corinthians:
"Love is patient and kind;
it is never jealous; love is never
boastful; it is never conceited; it is never rude
or selfish; it does not take offense,
and is not resentful.

"Love takes no pleasure in other people's
sins but delights in the truth; it is always
ready to excuse, to trust, to hope,
and to endure whatever comes.

"Love does not come to an end."

Such is love.
It is love between spouses and friends,
between Christ and his Church
and between God and you.
Ponder these lines,
put them into the mouth of God
spoken to you.
Can you accept that?
Can you accept that God is patient and kind
toward you;
that his love does not take offense
or hold grudges
toward you;
that his love
for you

is always ready to excuse, trust and hope,
to endure whatever comes?
Can you hear and hold to be true
for you
that God's love never comes to an end?

This is the message,
this is God as he reveals himself to us.
The question is not so much
"Does he work?"
as "Do we want this God
who loves us and demands one thing in
      return —
our love of him?"

Who is your God?

QUESTION 2
What Do You Seek?

FINDING the real God
means we must seek the real God,
which is a matter of asking the
right questions.
It means dealing with the question of
accepting the love of God.
And to accept love
rather than merely comply with
law, ritual and tradition
means that I do indeed ask something of
this God.
But what?
What is the question that
God is the answer to?

God's game is freedom.
The question is, if I truly seek
the freedom of the children of God,
this entails a willingness to let go of my
slavery, my death, my games and ego trips.
God does not participate in game-playing.
He, rather, is the source of the joyful hope of
     living
that arises from a union with
the Christ who rose from the dead, drawing all
things (like us) to himself.
Do we seek life within the Spirit of God,
is that what we ask for?
Is that what we really want?
If so, then God works.
If not,
we don't seek God.
Not really,
for we do not seek our
free selves and that is precisely
God's game.

Most Christians today are aware of the
    personage
of Mother Teresa of Calcutta.
Most know her work deals with
"the poorest of the poor."
Her institutes include homes for the
destitute dying,
houses for lepers,
homes for infants who have been abandoned
or simply those not wanted.
But her institutes,
her good works,
aren't what is so striking about this woman.
It is something else.
She recently visited this country,
speaking at conventions and churches.
She walked out on the stage.
Before she ever spoke a word,
the word she was spoke loudly.
Two days after the event the woman
telling me of it was in tears.
She was at the time as well.
She was sitting between two men
with her head riveted forward.
She didn't want the men to see for fear
they would think she was acting like a
"typical, silly woman."
I mean, what was there to cry about?
But then she noticed tears
in both their eyes as well.
No one at the convention of hundreds
was the same after seeing Mother Teresa.
Her presence changed them,
it was filled with power.
She is a superior
"show-through" of God.

Doesn't God work?
It depends on what we ask for.
What had happened to Mother Teresa?
What wonder had she worked on that crowd
of educated, responsible people?
From where the power?
Periodically,
all too seldom, we enter the presence
of a "saint" — someone who truly is different,
whose life truly has been changed
in a wondrous direction.
The level of serenity and radiant light
leaves no possibility of confusing
authentic God-acceptance for
emotional evangelism or fringe religion.

Not everyone can be a Mother Teresa.
Nor should we try to be anyone else.
Such marvelous mysteries are the business
of God alone.
But if we are discussing finding God,
which is the flowering of
seeking him,
then much can be learned from reflecting on
his saints.
People like Mother Teresa.
Their mythology of God is clear and sound;
what they ask is genuine and sincere.
Mother Teresa does not say to God,
"Why not do something beautiful for me?"
but rather,
"Now, let us do something beautiful for God."
And that "something beautiful" is always
a loving act for someone else,
flowing from her love of God.

Let us make a kind of
split screen of our consciousness,
on one half placing the extremely simple,
earthy but otherworldly face of
Mother Teresa.
On the other half is the often complex,
material, manipulating and manipulated face
of the rest of us.
As the "cameras" grind away,
giving us in stark contrast the difference,
several things become quite clear:
We are asking for two different things,
usually from two different motives.
Mother Teresa does not bargain with God.
She is not coming to him for solutions to
personal predicaments.
But an exchange has been made;
business has been carried out.
It is God's business,
God's game.
She has committed herself to surrendering her
slavery
for her Lord's freedom.

What is it that we seek from God?

The other side of the screen is quite different.
Here we most often see people trying to strike
      up a
bargain with God. You do this for me and
I will do that for you.
What is it that we ask of God?
Whatever it is, the request will clearly reflect
our mythology of this Lord of the universe.

Mike
comes clearly to mind;
his face is squarely in the slot opposite
Mother Teresa.
I know Mike well:
He is above average intellectually,
goes to a good college,
has a bright future
but
is lazy as an old log.
I vividly recall how happy he was with God
on one occasion.
He had not studied for an exam
and knew big trouble was in the wind
if he did poorly on the test.
What else is God for?
He struck up a bargain,
". . . Help me and
I will go to Mass every weekend for a month."
He bowed to this idol.
As it turned out,
he did well.
Nothing in the world could convince him
that it wasn't God
pulling strings for him;
until next time when
he doesn't do well.
Then God will be in trouble
with Mike.

God who?
What do we ask?

Terry is older
but not much different.
He is a good husband and father,
a proficient provider.
The trouble is when he is selling
on the road, he has this character defect:
He is usually unfaithful to his wife.
When I spoke to him he had just quit the
        Church.
He was outraged,
frustrated, disappointed and just plain
mad.
There he was, sitting in the doctor's office
fearing the worst — venereal disease.
Enter God.
Terry began to pray.
In exchange for a clean bill of health
he would give more to the Church,
say some prayers,
join the men's club
and go to Communion more often.
His bill of health wasn't clean.
And of course it was
God's fault.
God didn't work.
He was through with his game.

He was deaf to the fact that it
wasn't God's game
he was through with because
he had never started that.
What he was through with was the idol
of God he tried to manipulate
into playing his game.

He couldn't (wouldn't)
hear that God's game would be for him,
in honesty,
to admit and deal with his dishonoring
the marriage bond,
that "getting caught" could well be a
sacrament of God's love and mercy,
that this might be his "Kairos," his
moment of grace to exchange his slavery
for God's freedom.
His answer was there.
All that was lacking was the correct question.

It might be tempting for us to look at our
split screen
and say, "Well, sure,
those examples are extreme,
real but extreme.
What do they have to do with me?"
But in so saying, perhaps miss
that all our faces could at times
fit into the same square of screen.
We become so locked into our
bad mythology
we fail to see what it is that is being asked
at all.
Religion simply
doesn't work for many and there are good
        reasons.
We have often forgotten what it is all about:
freedom.

FREEDOM

Personal freedom
is no easy matter.
Not that it cannot be had;
the difficulty rather is that all too many people
don't want authentic freedom;
it is too hard.
The famous section from
Brothers Karamazov
on the Grand Inquisitor tells us clearly of this
condition.
The Church, which Dostoevsky hated,
symbolized by the Grand Inquisitor, proclaims
    to
Christ
that the people don't want freedom.
It is too heavy a burden for them.
They would rather lay their freedom
at the Church's feet like sheep, declares
the Inquisitor.
We love them enough to allow them to
surrender their freedom.
It is too much for them.
Christ,
on the other hand, is condemned precisely
    because
he lacks love for the people.
This is proven because he tells them
to take up their freedom,
to become their free selves,
to leave the chains of the slave.
He exhorts them to stand before the world
    and shout,
"I AM."

Such is precisely what Christ does
tell us.
But do we want our freedom?

One of the terrible prices of freedom
is the honesty to name our slavery.
How we dread this!
We dread it so much we hang on our cross
even though it is possible to
exchange it for joyful, if restless, freedom.
No child of God can
shake off the slave's chains if
he or she won't see where they are.

Freedom
is to be free of compulsion.
To be really free is to face several options,
knowing any one can be taken.
But many unnamed things compel us
to choose in slavery, not freedom.
God's game is setting us free.

For the sake of our discussion
let us pick three slaveries
that often go unnamed —
three slaveries that are not God's game:
fear, insecurity and habit.

Fear compels people to conform.
What we often conform to we don't want,
but we choose it nonetheless,
thus robbing us of our freedom.
We don't say this, of course;
we don't name it that,
thus, not naming it, we don't deal with it.
We don't surrender it to the loving power of
      God
and thus it retains its hold,
its bondage,
over us.

It may well be the last thing in the world
I want to do is
drink, or gossip about this person,
be unfaithful or cheat.
But I do.
Everyone else does, so I do.
Of course I call it by another name;
I call it being cool or tough.
It is okay to be cool or tough,
it is not okay to be controlled by fear.
And the storm rages, the waves toss,
reminiscent of another storm on another lake,
and the question is one of going it alone
or surrendering to a loving God.
That is a real question
with a real answer.

Fear
enslaves in so many ways.
It keeps people from accepting life
as a joy, as a profession;
it keeps them from trying new, exciting things,
from offering their opinions
in discussions,
from pouring new ideas into
their "old wineskins";
and so often it goes misnamed.

The way of Christ is
the way of freedom.
It is the way of surrendering slavery,
our special brand of slavery.
To accept love is to accept
that God won't fail us,
as long as he is God and not an idol
and as long as it is his game,
which is our *freedom,*
and not merely our comfort.
Do we really want God?
Do we want to surrender our slavery?

Fear
is the greatest inhibitor of communication.
So many will live and die
never having said the things
that are most important,
never having said "I'm sorry"
when they were,
never having reached out to someone
when they desperately wanted to.
Perhaps the vast majority of our fellow humans
have no one in their lives,
not even their spouses,
whom they trust enough to share their
weakness with,
share their dreams and fears with,
share their hopes with.
Why?
Again, most often we misname it;
that way we don't have to deal with it.
We say, "No one cares,"
or "They won't understand." We say,
"It isn't worth bothering someone with."
Isn't it?
If it isn't worth bothering with,
then why did Christ come to earth?
What else, then, was he speaking of
when he promised all who would follow
". . . abundant life"?

Fear enslaves.
To find God is to find our
free self;
which is a matter of exchanging our slavery
for God's power setting us free.

Insecurity
is a form of fear,
crippling vast numbers of our brothers and
        sisters.
Perhaps more than anything else, it deals with
competition.
If I am not satisfied with myself,
then all that is left is competition with
someone else.
Everyone is a threat to me,
perhaps even my spouse and children.
The very thought of dealing with this
ball-and-chain
is so frightening, so horrendous,
we refuse to allow it into our conscious mind.
We say our prayers,
beg for a good turnout at our card party or
family picnic,
but never think of laying our insecurity
before the power of God.
What is it then that we ask
of God?

Freedom is lack of compulsion.
How many new cars are gotten,
new boats obtained,
new sets of clothes bought,
diets undertaken,
little-known facts sprung at parties,
not out of freedom but out of the need to
impress?

To let everyone know I am as big
a big shot
as they?
I have to keep up by going out to eat
as often,
go to as many shows,
have as many new friends,
because if I don't,
"they" will have the edge.
Who are "they"?

Competition seeps into everything.
Church activity is undertaken,
at times
not out of a commitment and expression of
     love
but to
not fall behind my neighbor, Jack.
We end up having to prove ourselves
to everyone,
most of whom couldn't care less,
and thus we end up in an endless cycle of
proving ourselves to ourselves.
And there is no freedom.

But God's game *is* our freedom.
The question isn't if he has the power
or the concern,
it is if we have the desire to be free
of our slavery.
If not, then
no,
God doesn't work.
But then it isn't God
we seek.

Of course the obvious point is not
that new cars, clothes or little-known facts
are evil.
The point in question is the motivation behind
        their
presence.
The point is our personal freedom,
our personal surrender to a loving God
who alone counts anyway
and who has declared that we
are just fine with him.

Living within the insensitivity of habit
is its own special brand of inner blindness.
We become so accustomed to inner darkness,
to the same old grind,
the same old streets, same people, same job,
that we miss most of what is there.
We fail to see the ice
making magic art on the power lines,
miss the flowers of the fields,
the innocence lost or preserved in the
face of a child.
In short, we arrive at the point of death where
nothing matters much.
Rather than name this
laziness or simply not caring, we say,
"There is nothing to care about,"
while all around us people bleed and die,
are born and cease to move among us.
And all the while the face of
Mother Teresa
on the other side of the screen
beams at us with the power of someone who
        has
totally
desired to be free of the chains,
someone who has surrendered to Love,
who has found and embraced the
Covenant God.
The exchange has been made.

EXCHANGE

And again my mind is a stage
across which pass many people
seeking God, whether they know it or not.
They have confused God with idols.
There was a great mountain climber who
fell off the cliff,
surely to his death.
But there was the branch sticking
out of the mountainside.
He grabbed it and,
what else,
began to pray.
Imagine his joy when a rumbling voice
    boomed,
"This is God — what can I do for you?"
The response seemed obvious to the dangling
    climber:
"Save me!"
His mythology being what it was,
he began to strike a bargain.
"If you do," he said,
"I will go to church more often,
help the Boy Scouts and be a lector at Mass."
God retorted,
"Yes, fine, but do you love me?"
At this point the climber would say he loved
anyone.
"Certainly, but please hurry, the branch is
    breaking."
"Do you trust me?" asked God.
"Of course I do," said the frightened man.
"Everyone knows you can do anything."

"Then I will save you," said God.
"All you have to do is one thing."
"Name it!" shouted the man.
"Let go of the branch."
There was a long pause,
very long,
then the man shouted out over the cliff,
"Is anyone else up there?"

Freedom requires an exchange,
a giving up of one thing for another.
To find God is to attempt the exchange.
The degree we find God
is the degree we surrender
to the exchange;
we only find God by
allowing him to
have us, which is to
set us free.
Not free of pain but
free of slavery.
We might view the elements of the exchange
    in this manner:
exchanging dishonesty for honesty,
pride for humility
and reliance upon our own power for depen-
    dence on
a loving God.

We have spoken much of honesty already.
If I can reduce God to some silly idol
whom I can manipulate with some prayers
or a few dollars or good works,
then I don't have to take him seriously.
A god subject to man is hardly a
god to be concerned with.
But if in honesty I truly reflect on scripture
and the word as it lives and fights for life
in me,
then a different God emerges.
He then is a God who demands growth,
who will not pour his "new wine"
into the wine sacks we dishonor.

HELP ME

"Help me"
are the first words toward finding God.
Help me be free,
help me deal with my own slavery,
help me shuck off my compulsions —
help me.
But how difficult those two words
when said honestly.
How it goes against the grain to admit
we need help,
to admit our corners of hell,
to acknowledge there is a PERSONAL God
concerned with my personal freedom.
What else can show us our
hidden immaturities,
our boulder-like character defects
but the light of honesty?
Childish temper tantrums hiding
as righteous indignation
must be named;
fear of love hiding
as "too cool to be caught"
must be seen for what it is;
inability to accept love wearing the mask of
sophistication
must be illuminated in the glare of honesty
before we can deal with it at all.
Only in the exchange of honesty for
dishonesty will we ever come to the altar of
     God
and find him there
rather than an idol.

Pride for humility
demands that we cease the blasphemous
        charade
of pretending we are no good.
The very fact that we have been
". . . bought by the blood of Christ"
speaks of our dignity and worth.
Yet
"I'm worthless," has often worn the name
of humility.
Rather
the essence of humility might be summed up
in what has come to be called the serenity
        prayer:
"God, grant me the serenity to accept
what I cannot change; the courage to
change what I can and the wisdom
to know the difference."
It is a matter of knowing our limits,
knowing what can be changed
and accepting that all good things
are possible with the surrender to God.

With us, as with Mother Teresa,
there are many things we cannot change.
Were she able to wipe out poverty,
disease, destitutes dying on the street,
she would.
But she cannot.
There are those things in life that
must be accepted.
Pride demands,
in its ego-centered blindness,
"I can change all things
and do it instantaneously."
Those things I cannot change,
declares pride,
I will not accept.
To find God, an exchange must be made.

At times we lament,
"If only I would have said something
or done something different,
this evil thing wouldn't have happened."
But we do not sit at the
right hand of God.
It is not our game, our show —
it is God's.
Not to accept what is unchangeable
breeds frustration, anger and rage.
Humbly asking God for the grace to
accept what cannot be changed breeds
tranquility of spirit, hope and peace.
And such are exactly the qualities of one
making an exchange with God.

But there are those things we
can change.
We do have control over such qualities as
self-pity, jealously and greed.
We are masters of the degree of
happiness we allow ourselves to enjoy
in this life.

On the same street we meet the man
with no legs
happily, serenely going about his business
and the man with tight shoes
cursing life with all his might.
We meet a Mother Teresa
living with abject poverty and with serenity
and the man in utter turmoil of spirit
because he can't afford a new car this year.
We meet the drinking alcoholic
and the brother recovering from alcohol.
One says, "I have every reason to be
miserable,"
and the other answers, "Yes, but only because
you wish to be."

The question is, are we willing to
exchange,
to surrender our slavery for God's freedom?
The wisdom to know the difference
is no little gift.
It is, again, a matter of knowing the right
questions to ask.
You cannot change the fact of a divorce,
but you can deal creatively with loneliness;
you cannot make yourself taller if you are
    short,
but you can deal with the hostility generated
    by
insensitive people joking about it;
you cannot make a person who is dead live
    again,
but you can do something about the despair
such an event may cause in your life.
What is the question: can God
reverse what has happened?
Or can he give me the spiritual power to deal
with what is
and thus make of its pain the catalyst
of growth?
God cannot protect us from pain
but the God of Easter can and
passionately desires
to lead us through that pain to greater life.

To possess God is to be
possessed by him. It is to
exchange the priority of things material
for things spiritual.
It is not to become heavenly as opposed to
earthly but to create
here and now
the kingdom of God among the children of
    men.

None of this, of course, is possible
by ourselves.
Thus the two basic words,
"Help me."
God, who is beyond my own limits,
help me;
God, who knows how weak I am,
help me;
God, who is aware of my fear,
help me.
We have tried so often alone,
only to discover our own limitations.
But just this message is the
word of God:
You don't have to do it alone.
"I will be with you all days . . ."

With you for what?
To accomplish what?
To bring what into being?
The natural question arising
at this point is
one of commitment.
How badly do we wish to risk freedom
and thus find the God of life?
This is a key consideration.

There is not only that point
beyond which I cannot go myself
but that point where I must make a
decision, a conversion
about what it is I do seek.

Such phrases as,
"Let the dead bury the dead," ". . . any man
     who
puts his hand to the plow and keeps looking
     back
is not worthy of the kingdom," ". . . the luke-
     warm I
will vomit from my mouth,"
should rattle us to the bone.
There is no compromise in these words.

The exchange, the growth in freedom
cannot be total and instantaneous.
Bad habits and old ways of acting
cut deep into our beings.
We did not get sick all at once;
we will not be cured all at once.
God does not expect such unrealistic results.
Only man flogs man with the insanity of
     perfection.

Once we have broken our idols
and sought freedom rather than a
perpetuation of slavery,
we
hear our God whisper in our hearts,
"Go slow,
be patient,
allow me to work in you,
allow me to become you.
You are my pearl
and I have set the value as priceless."

QUESTION 3
How Do You Seek?

SOME WOULD SAY of our meditation thus
far,
"Perhaps it does make sense—but—
it is too hard.
If this is what the God of love asks,
it is too much.
Don't you understand how
terrified
I am of my fear?
Don't you realize how
difficult it would be to
give up my games?
They are all I have.
I'm not a Mother Teresa or a
saint; I need some fun."
But fun isn't the question.
One of the most pitiful, heartrending
statements I've ever heard was said
by a woman in a meeting.
She was telling of a mild confrontation
with her alcoholic spouse.
"Sure we drink too much," he admitted,
"both of us. But what would we do if
we didn't? What else is there?"
What is there,
he was saying, to take the place
of our tranquilizer?
How else can we cope with life?
Is there anything else to living?
Not admitting the option,
there was no option.

But there are other things.
There are other things to replace our
fear, insecurity and deadly habit of living.
There is something better.
There is loving involvement with other
human beings,
there are genuine communication and trust,
there are loving and being loved,
there are caring and sharing.
And there is God's game,
freedom.

Our hesitation in
claiming God as our God
often originates in our fear of
what would we do without our games.
If I don't talk about myself incessantly,
no one will notice me;
if I don't grab for myself,
no one will give me a thing;
if I don't pity myself, you can bet
 no one else will.
If I don't build up walls
protecting me from loneliness,
even if they are tranquilizers
that demon will tear me
limb from limb—
so what else is there beyond these
limitations I have surrounded myself with?
That is a valid question admitting of
an honest answer: exchange,
God.

No one ever said it was easy
or comfortable.
But then neither is the slow death of slavery.
It is no simple matter to smash our idol
if in fact that is what our God has become.
It is terrifying even to consider
surrendering to the Real,
acknowledging that we open ourselves
to the risk of freedom,
to the light of honesty.
No journey threatens with more dangers
or promises more hideous demons—
and none offers such a rich reward.

None of it happens fast;
there is no instant cure for heartache.
And none of it can happen at all without
a program and a caring community.
Once the idol has been named and
the road of freedom along which the God
of life can be found is undertaken,
then there is the need for a program.

"If you want a piece of the rock,"
said a great man,
"you must go where the rock is."
Ever so many of the people who have said
in one form or another,
"God doesn't work,"
have never gone to the rock.
They complain in immense pain of confusion,
depression, problems:
They are having marriage problems,
family problems,
personal problems.

Beyond the matters of commitment and
bad mythology are the questions,
when was the last time you prayed,
the last time you quietly reflected or
read anything of value?
Is there anyone you share with?
Anyone you talk to in order that your
insights may be deepened,
your journey supported and challenged?
More often than not there is
no answer to these queries.
They are not interested in these
"secondary things"; what they are concerned
     with
is instant results
which means release from pain
rather than spiritual growth.

Anyone who would begin or remain
in the way of Christ
which is the way of freedom needs a program.
The possibility of self-deception and
apathy is too great
without a workable program.
This is true of the Holy Father,
Mother Teresa and the thousands of
little people
who would follow in the way of Christ.
But how often we miss this point.
After reading material like the
preceding chapters, we may be enthused—
yes, we will surrender to God,
we will name our demons and choose
freedom over slavery,
we will let the divine light shine in us
and through us.
Yes, we will:
How?

There we stop.
Days elapse, months go by
and soon we not only have not started
but have forgotten what we were going to
        start.
Whenever the ideas of God over idol
appear in our minds we quickly
sink them;
"We tried that,
it doesn't work."

It does work,
but only with a program . . .
A program—your program.
Why we overlook this important aspect of
spiritual growth is hard to see.
We acknowledge the need of a program in
        other areas of
our living
but not in the realm of growth
in spiritual freedom.
Anyone starting a diet knows
there are times to eat and times you can't;
there are certain things allowed
and other things that aren't.
An exchange is demanded here too.
To violate the program is to
eliminate the chance of achieving the goal.

Any youth involved in sports is aware
of the need of a program.
There are practice times.
To miss practice means you don't want to win
very badly
and therefore should quit playing the game
as if you did.

Sacrifice and commitment are
called for.
Many things, good things,
that could be done after school
are given up.
The aspiring athlete has
chosen something else.
There are techniques to be learned,
skills acquired only through doing it
over and over,
again and again until it becomes a
way of life.

The same is true of a student.
Studying when you feel like it
accomplishes little.
Those who acquire the "habit of study"
are the ones who become truly educated.
Habits are learned by repeated acts.
What is not repeated does not become
part of me.
What I do not make a part of me
is not important to me.
Finding God is a matter of choosing a
way of life.
This way can only be maintained by
repeated acts.
Repeated acts become a way of life when
    incorporated
into a program.

The process of freedom is just that,
a process.
It is the result of an initial decision
and countless other decisions
made many times a day.
We have a choice to say
a kind or ugly word,
to smile or frown,

to be in competition with someone or not,
to confront our own feelings of false guilt
and unworthiness or let these demons possess
      us.
Finding God is not a
once-and-for-all kind of thing.
It is rather like a sunrise:
never the same
yet always beautiful.

There is no one program.
It is not a matter of comparing mine
with yours and judging mine as better
because I am doing more.
That is idol talk.
Love is not a matter of technique or
      competition,
it is rather a surrender to truth.
The important thing about a program is
that it fits you
and that it exists.

Nor is it a matter of making the program
the center of your God-discovery.
Just as law can replace God
on the altar of love,
so can we make an idol of the very
program by which we hope to find God.
The program is not the goal;
the progressive discovery of God is.
It is possible to rigidify a program to the
      extent

that it no longer serves
the purpose for which it was created.
We could find ourselves, for example,
in a neurotic sweat to "get our prayers in"
when we are too tired or sick
to do anything but surrender ourselves to God
just as we are.
But such is not the purpose of the program
in the first place.
Honesty will be the guide.

The elements of a program are like small
      stones
tucked around the base of a boulder.
The boulder is our "demon";
it is the major obstacle to our growth,
to our exchange with God, our holiness.
The task is to keep the boulder from
tearing loose and
rampaging down the hill destroying
all that was built.
Working our program keeps the boulder in
      place,
out of the way,
so that we may journey around it.
As long as the stones stay in place there
will be no avalanche.
It is not really possible to slip;
slips are planned.
Sometimes, in the darkness of dishonesty,
we plan them for months or years.
We begin by inching out the pebbles.
Prayer slackens and
becomes insincere; it becomes idol talk.
We say it is no big thing.
We stop reading, saying
we are too busy.
That too is "no big thing."
Slowly we cut out all
quiet
in our lives.

We replace reflection with noise or
busywork.
We lose sight of who we are or
where we are—
which is what the pebble-pulling was
about all the time.

Now the disaster is ready to
suddenly
befall us.
We are accidents in search
of a place to happen.
Someone says something or
we provoke a scene, then angrily shout,
"That's it! That's all
I can take. I deserve my demon."
And choosing the demon, we reap the
fruits of the demon: misery.
It was no accident.
We made ourselves unhappy and promptly
    blamed
someone else—probably God.
"Why did he let this happen?"

But what should your program be?
One man's program is another's prison.
Let us suggest that
whatever form yours takes, it includes these
elements:
(1) prayer; (2) reflection; (3) sharing.
These "pebbles" must be fitted
to each one's life and day;
they all must be undertaken before the face
of your loving God and not an angry idol;
these are not ways to manipulate God
but to open us up to his way for our life,
which is abundant life.

PROGRAM: Prayer

Saying prayers is an essential element
of a prayerful life.
The prayers *are not* the prayerful life
but manifestations of it.
Diamonds are not the diamond mine;
they are only expressions of its wealth.
Just so it is with praying.
A prayerful life is one
open to the Spirit,
one free to respond to God as he speaks
to us day by day.
That cannot be without conscious contact.
To want the rock is to go to the rock.

It seems unthinkable that two lovers
would spurn talking to each other.
Words are often the wings of love,
just as they are the wings of hatred.
It *is* important in many ways
that we verbalize what we think and feel.
Not only that the "other" may know
but that we may, in speaking, come to a
    deeper
knowledge of what we mean as well.

Speaking to God, of course, need not
be a matter of formal, organized words.
But it does not exclude them either.
What the words are is of
secondary importance to their motivation.

For some the Morning Offering is a
soulful, genuinely spiritual beginning
of each day.
Others would find this unthinkably formal.
Some are lucky to find their coffee cup
for the first hour, let alone "say a prayer."
The important consideration is not what it is
but that it is.

I vividly recall a young bearded Chicagoan
sitting on a cement pier jutting out into
Lake Michigan
one summer morning.
He was quietly sitting there
awaiting the rising sun.
When it first made its appearance over the
water's edge,
he stood and began playing his saxophone.
It must have taken the sun a full 15 minutes
to make its appearance;
it was serenaded the full time.
Could that not have been
possibly
a magnificent morning offering?

Conscious contact is the thing.
Or "raising your heart and mind to God,"
if that suits you better.
Whatever the terminology and
whenever it occurs during the day,
it must be honest, sincere and free.
Above all, it must be.

Perhaps there are some today who would see
daily or frequent Mass and the sacrament of
        Reconciliation
as passe.
"That is pre-Vatican II," they would say,
"it is superstition, out of date."
Is it?
Is it not again a matter of mythology?
Assuredly any of the sacraments
can be reduced to superstition,
daily Mass or weekends.
It is very true that Mass,
daily or otherwise,
cannot bribe God; it is not a tool
of manipulation.

But if freedom is what we seek
and God is the Real
into whom we seek entrance, then
loving communication through this
endless mystery of love,
which is what the Eucharist is,
certainly does work.

Holiness is a word naming the
exchange of slavery for freedom.
That is what the word means.
In the Eucharistic liturgy we say,
". . . All life, all holiness comes from you
through your Son, Jesus Christ."
That is correct, Christian mythology.
Eucharist is for the worship of the Father,
which is our holiness.
Holiness is the process of exchange.
To see the Eucharist in this light
makes it a center of power, a source of light,
and who is there among us not in need of
power and light?
That is,
if it is freedom we seek.

Penance is also a question of
mythology.
If it is to us a
"telling of our sins so
we can get to heaven," and that alone,
then we have seriously missed the meaning
of the sacrament.
Sins are sins because they are
a rejection of freedom,
an embracing of darkness.
St. Paul flatly says,
"Before grace there was no sin";
without love there is no sin.

Sin is the rejection of a loving relationship.
Heaven,
and we cannot know the "what" of heaven
any more than we can know the is-ness of
     God,
is the full attainment of love
and thus freedom.
The sacrament of Reconciliation does not deal
merely with "sin" as we understand that
     term—
that is, the breaking of an arbitrary law.
It has to do with gaining perspective on our
exchange, on our desire for growth;
it has to do with naming our demon;
it has to do with quietly identifying our
degree of exchange with God;
it has to do with the serious question of
whether we worship an idol or God.

We used to think,
not wholly without cause,
that the reason it took great courage to
"go to confession"
was the questionable temperament of the
     priest.
That may still be true.
But a deeper reason for courage is
the demand for the honesty reconciliation
     necessitates.
Honesty not only to see
what I have done,
but where I am and who I am.
I am
a child of God, loved by God.

I am called forth to accept this truth,
to embrace this mystery,
to remove the obstacles that keep this
reality from being real.
Am I?
Can I?
Do I?
Such are the questions of Penance.

Your program is for the sake of
God-consciousness; it is a question of
spiritualizing your entire life.
Ohiyesa, a Santee Dakota Indian speaking in
     1911,
said this of his people's God-consciousness:
"In the life of the Indian there
was only one inevitable duty—
the duty of prayer, the daily recognition
of the Unseen and Eternal.
Each soul must meet the morning sun,
the new sweet earth and the Great Silence
     alone.
Whenever in the course of the daily hunt
the red hunter comes upon a scene
strikingly beautiful or sublime—
a black thundercloud with the rainbow's
     glowing
arch above the mountain, a white waterfall
in the heart of the green gorge; a vast prairie
     tinged
with the blood-red of sunset . . .
he pauses for an instant in the attitude of
     worship.
He sees no need for setting apart
one day in seven as holy,
since all days are God's."

Perhaps they were a more God-conscious
        people
than we.

Pick your time,
time that fits *your* day whoever you are:
When you rise and retire,
before the first class,
just before the kids come home from school,
just before the first service call of the day—
whenever.
And do it.
Contact your God.
It doesn't mean you can't pray at other times;
just don't neglect conscious contact at these
        special times.

PROGRAM: Reflection

Of all aspects of a program, perhaps
this is the most difficult.
We are so conditioned that doing is good
we find it hard to "do nothing" but
quietly reflect.
Reflection demands inner silence
just as honesty demands reflection.
It is again a question of mythology.
In effect we say countless times in our society,
"If you produce, you are good—if not,
you are useless."
But what of the retired? What of the
physically handicapped, the retarded?
What of the unborn?
All too often our real question is,
"Well, what do they do?"
They live;
is that not sufficient?
Life, as Browning told us of beauty,
 is its own reason for being.

It is in prayerful reflection that
the Word who is God speaks to the
words that we are.
Only in this "bending back" do we know
what and who is around us.
Minus reflection, Eucharist degenerates
into merely "eating the host."
Penance shrinks to just
"telling our sins,"
God becomes the Law
or the super Valium pill
and our slavery remains a constant condition.
Without reflection, we discover no
new meaning
and thus are powerless to change our
bad mythologies into anything more
        authentic.

Our word "angel" comes from an ancient
     word
meaning messenger.
Messenger is what the word means in
     scripture.
In our ultrapragmatic, literal Western mind
we demand that "angels" look like something.
So we concocted tall, feathery creatures,
to fill the meaning.
These angels give us messages from God,
protect us and send Satan
(a word meaning adversary) into hell.
Some people say that such creatures,
spiritual beings who are yet not God,
do not exist.
What scripture tells us is that God speaks
to his people.
It tells us that there are indeed
"angelos," messengers of God, all around us.
There are people, scenes,
events and incidents all around that
speak of and would raise our minds to God.
Have you seen any angels today?

If not, it is not because
they were not in your world,
but that lacking a reflective skill,
you were not aware of them.
The rising of the sun,
the innocence or hardness of a child's face,
the blue of the sky and
wrinkles of an aged person's face . . .
all are angels.
All reveal, to the spiritually sighted,
the story of God becoming man that
"all things may be new."

Let us again hear from
Chief Luther Standing Bear:
". . . the man who sat on the ground of
his tipi, meditating on life and its meaning,
accepting the kinship of all creatures
and acknowledging unity with the universe,
was infusing into his being the true essence of
civilization.
And when native man left off this form
of development,
his humanization was retarded in growth."
There really can be no prayer
without reflection;
nor reflection that cannot be a prayer.
Time for one
in a program may be time for both.
But it is also possible to say words,
calling them prayers,
without reflective meaning.
Or to reflect as if God has no part
in all the efforts of growth.
Together they constitute a kiss;
standing alone they constitute
kissing yourself.

PROGRAM: Sharing

Reflection might be hard
but it is not repulsive.
It is not frightening because it is done
in private. It is personal.
Sharing is something else.
It *is* frightening because it is not
done in private.
Sharing demands I verbalize
to another human being
where I am and who I am.
It is a matter of getting what is
inside outside.
And here is where so many
jump off the program.
They are willing to work it alone
but don't ask them to
share it with anyone else
because that means sharing me
and that I won't do.

Why should sharing be a
part of a person's program?

If we see holiness as exchange
and exchange as freedom, then
growth is the outcome.
The trouble is, we scarcely know what
spiritual growth means.
We did not become who we were alone,
we did not become broken alone
and we will not become healed alone.
It happens within the context of
community.

Without sharing, without
this inclusion into a community which
both supports and challenges,
it is too easy to fool ourselves.
The community prohibits us from
not naming or misnaming what is.
What is inside and remains so is unseen.
What we think we see or know may
turn out to
be something quite different when
we verbalize it to another.
"Who do men say that I am?" asks Christ.
    "Who do you
say that I am?"
We think we know. Say it to another.
Then you will know if you know what
you think.
We think we know what we are looking for
in finding God.
Say it to another, verbalize it.
What do you seek?
In saying it you will know what
you don't understand.
We perhaps are absolutely certain that
we can accept love.
Reflect, think on it, talk about it.
Maybe you can't.
Not God's or man's.

But more than just clarification of ideas
is the matter of healing.
Love heals.
But love is not merely
IN
someone.
Love is a between kind of thing.
It happens between people,
it takes place in all the betweens of a
loving, believing community.
To discover that I am important,
that kindness is possible,
that I can trust and be trusted,
that God is the Real in love—
these are the elements of healing.
But each demands someone else.
How do I know gentle tenderness
is possible if I do not see it or am not the
recipient of this "smile of God."

Tormented,
possessed people glut our churches
and streets.
The stories and hurts,
if they were told, would wring
tears from a stone.
You cannot just bury a fear, pain or obsession
and have it go away.
All one does who proceeds with this attitude
is to bury the demon alive,
to give it a place to hide,
where it eats you from the inside out.

Oh, but we are so sure
there is no one to tell,
no one who will understand,
no one who cares.
I am too ugly to let anyone see;
if they did, I would be rejected forever
and that is precisely what I most fear.
To share would be to cut my own throat.

". . . if we didn't drink,
what would we do?"

Finding God is giving up games
in favor of truth.
Whatever we feel about our status of
        worthiness
in the eyes of others is ultimately
what we feel about our status before God.
There *are* people who care
and to share with.
That is not the problem.
The problem is with us—
it is that we cannot trust.

As risky and hard as it is,
there is perhaps no greater joy than the
freedom of finally being able to trust.
At that moment in faith
when I take that risk, saying,
"Help me,"
that terrible risk and say to a worthy,
well-chosen other,
"What I really feel is miserable,
or ugly, or lonely or afraid,"
then does God walk into our lives.
Not because before he would not,
but because we would not.

As one insightful minister put it,
"We need community on earth
to know what is going on in heaven."

This chapter is not a
surefire technique that,
if faithfully followed,
will deliver God into your hands.
It only states the need for a regular,
sane program of finding and continuing the
search for God.
Three elements of a program are suggested;
you must fit them into the mosaic of your day.
No one can work your program for you,
just as no one can find your God for you.
It is your program and your God.

4
So Be It

WITH THE EXCHANGE comes sight,
with sight comes a change of priorities;
often that which was not important
now is, that which was essential
now doesn't matter.
This finding of God,
this claiming of personal freedom,
does it matter?
Is it important?
In the grand scale of human commerce
and "big deals,"
is it of importance that someone,
anyone,
finds his way off the idol altar
and into the temple of God?

That is a question each must decide
for himself.

Clarence Darrow is a name
many will no longer remember even though
he was one of, if not the,
greatest defense attorneys in American history.
Being an avowed agnostic,
it might seem strange for his name to turn
      up here,
in a religious book.
Stranger still
is to see his name linked at all
with Mother Teresa of Calcutta.
Yet there are similarities.
Clarence Darrow, like Mother Teresa,
made an exchange in his life.

Not an exchange that took place all at once,
or made from the same motive as the
saint of Calcutta,
but one that set his life apart
all the same.
Mr. Darrow could have sold out.
With his genius and gifts of
persuasion
he could have possessed great power
as we usually speak of power.
He could have been rich
and the pet of the jet set.
He was none of these things.

Like Mother Teresa, and anyone in the way
of finding the Covenant God,
he pitched his tent among men.
Compassion was chosen over riches,
commitment over fame,
involvement over apathy.

He too collected destitutes—
the people of the night
from the streets.
It was told of a poor Black man
who came to him for help over an eviction:
Darrow asked, "How much money do you
      have?"
Dejectedly the man turned to leave,
confident that now there would be no help.
"None," he said.
The lawyer's response was,
"Well, in that case, I guess
I'll have to defend you."
Such was the vision,
the angel-listening, of the man.

Darrow was as powerful with a pen as
in swaying a jury.
He wrote two short stories that
have their place here:
"The Breaker Boy," which appeared in the
Chicago Evening American in 1902,
and "Little Louis Epstein," which appeared in
the *Pilgrim* in 1903.

THE BREAKER BOY

"The Breaker Boy" starts with the telltale
        sentence,
"Johnny McCaffrey was eleven years old
when he became a man."
It is the familiar story of a poverty-stricken
Irish family who comes to America
seeking a better way of life.
They settle in Scranton, Pennsylvania.
Owen, the father, immediately begins
working in the mine; he becomes a slave
to the company, buying at their store,
living in their house, using their goods.
When he is killed in the mine,
Johnny becomes a man.
Each morning, with the other boys, he climbs
the mountain of slag or "culm."
Once at the top, he straddles an iron chute,
down which shoots the mined coal mixed with
        jagged
pieces of slate.
The boy's job is to snatch out the slate
as it shoots past.

Dense clouds of coal dust
engulf everything on the culm mountain;
not infrequently blood is spilled on the coal.
"But then," says Darrow, "there is a little blood
on all our coal,
and most everything else we use."
Blood from some small breaker boy far up
the slag mountain.
Forty years John McCaffrey
has been a breaker boy, a door boy at the
        mine,
a driver, a helper, a miner and now
has come out of the mine to spend his last
        few years
above ground.

The mine has changed him.
His face is scarred, one ear is missing
from a belated powder blast,
one arm is crippled from a falling rock and his
right hip is never free from the pain of
rheumatism.
Of course, like all miners he has developed
the black lung, asthma,
which allows him to walk only a few steps
without the terrible wheezing starting.

The crew boss was not a bad man;
he did what he could for John.
Nor was Mr. Fox, the mine owner, an evil
     person.
It just never occurred to him that there was
anything wrong with what happened to John
     McCaffrey,
that men spent their lives in death-trap mines.

There is no big event in John's life that
changes all of this.
He is not promoted to mine supervisor
nor does he marry the owner's daughter.
But then, often life offers no fairy-tale events
     either.
The story ends with John again,
slowly and painfully, ascending the mountain
to seek his seat with the ever-new, young
     children.
"Then," as Mr. Darrow concludes,
"he took his rheumatic leg in his
hand, raised his foot until it rested
on the right side of the long chute;
then he raised his left foot to
the other side,
bent over and looked down at the black iron
trough, and waited for the coal to rumble
     down."

LITTLE LOUIS EPSTEIN

Little Louis Epstein
is the same boy, only with a different face,
different city and different name.
He is the same because the same ugly,
blind forces that shattered the life of
John McCaffrey also twisted his fate.
Louis lived on Maxwell Street in Chicago.
He too was poor and helped his family by
selling papers.
Besides the poverty, however, Louis had
another handicap—he had but one hand
due to a street accident.
Louis was nine years old.

Even at that tender age the little boy
understood how loving his mother was;
he noticed how much she gave up for things
    to be nice
for the rest of them.
He saw her fatigue and efforts to smile
and keep them cheerful.
Mostly he noticed she had nothing nice
to call her own.

Then he saw in the window of a large store
before which he sold his papers
a beautiful string of red stones.
Even though it cost the staggering sum of
forty-eight cents,
he made up his mind he would get it for his
    mother
for Christmas.

As the weeks went by
Louis held out a few pennies
whenever he could.
His mother must not know of the
splendid gift.
His boy's mind was afire with
happiness over the thought of
his mother's joy at having such a
beautiful thing to call her own.

Everyone remembered the 18th of December;
it was by far the coldest day of the year.
Louis' mother asked him not to go out that
        morning
but he would hear none of it.
She bundled him up in the warmest clothes
they had
and he set off.
He was glad it was cold;
many of the other paper sellers would stay
        home,
thus making it easier for him to make some
        extra pennies.
And he was almost ready to buy the red
        necklace.

Mr. Darrow is again at pains to stress
there is no evil creature,
no devil,
behind all of the situations influencing
the boy's life.
Louis' family is a unit of love,
the people he meets are generally good to
        him—
even if the floorwalker of a big store chases
        him
away this bitter cold day.

The floorwalker was once poor too, and Louis
is too young to know
"the man born in poverty and misfortune
almost always grows very hard,
unless he keeps his poverty and misfortune."

On this particular day, paper selling
has an added obstacle.
Usually Louis just held the unsold papers
under his handless arm
and made change with the other.
Being so cold on this day, however,
the hand making change is always exposed to
the wind.
At first it stings and hurts fearfully.
So much so, he considers giving up.
But he cannot,
then he might not be able to get the necklace;
perhaps someone else would buy it
in the meantime.
Suddenly his hand stops hurting.
In fact, there is a sensation of warmth.
The hand, of course, is frostbitten.
Louis' mother tries to get circulation going
when he gets home
but can't.
She fears the worst.
They rush to the hospital where all the people
are very nice and
Louis loses his remaining hand.
Nine is not very many years to have lived.

In response to his tears his mother comforts
      him:
His family will always love him, she says,
they will always take care of him.
He knows this;
this is not why he cries.
It is just that "it was so near Christmas
and he couldn't get the rest of the money.
She asked him what he meant,
and then between sobs he told her about the
      beads."

The content and outcome of these stories
are not pretty.
They were not meant to be.
Much in our world is not pretty.

There is, indeed,
"a little blood on all our coal."

The real tragedy about these stories
is not that they were
and are true
but that they came about because
good men were blind.
There is no archvillain,
no evil-intentioned madman.
The people—
us—
are not so much inclined to evil as
not inclined to spiritual growth.
Spiritual blindness resulting in
slavery,

freedom not chosen,
growth not undertaken,
God not claimed,
is too often the case.
To find God
is to find sight.
It is to be able to see the blood
on our coal.
John and Louis live all around us.
Sometimes in our sophistication
we grow very hard,
we become "realistic" and say to such misery,
"So be it."
So be it as if there were no other way
it could be.
But so be it can mean something else as well.
It can mean a surrender to love
rather than to slavery,
it can mean calling life from death rather
than letting life decay into death.
The direction is a choice,
the choice is ours.

We are physical, material men.
Being so, our world must necessarily be
tangible, concrete, visible.
But whatever form these
tangible, concrete, visible elements
of our world take, it is a direct
reflection
of the inner state of man.
Our world is the reflection,
mirrorlike,
of man's spirit.

If our laws, ethics, establishment,
cities, policies (both foreign and domestic)
have come to exist so that
all the John McCaffreys and Louis Epsteins
remain subject to inhuman conditions,
then it is so because
that is where our spirits are.
If
retirement and leisure have become
a major problem in our society,
it is not because we have so many
retirees
but because we have not the spirit within
    ourselves
and in our society to make of
"free time" an asset rather than a sentence
    of doom.
We know how to work but
perhaps not how to live.
If old age
has come to be a curse
because our society has no room or desire for
the long-lived,
it is a reflection of our poor vision,
our devaluation of the preciousness of life.
Whatever is unjust, inhuman
and degrading to the human spirit
in our physical society
had its birth in the spirit of men.

What is "out there"
is there because first of all it was
"in here."

If we are not dealing with spiritual progress
we are not dealing with the problems.
All the laws or "funding"
of history cannot make a Mr. Fox see the
breaker boy bleeding on his coal.
How many Louis Epsteins must lose their
second hand
before we floorwalkers stop chasing them
away from our doors?

What is at question here is not
reform laws
but spiritual freedom;
it is a matter of priorities
and priorities are a matter of who your God is
and what you are asking when you find him.
Jesus' question: "Who do you say that I am?"

The temptation is great in our
monetary society
to hire people to solve our problems,
to make them go away.
We employ city planners, lawyers and
        ministers
and say, "Do your job—
wipe the blood from our coal."
But it is our coal.
Money cannot cleanse it.
Education cannot wipe it clean.
Laws cannot take the stains away.
If we would really do something about
human misery,
we must be prepared to make the exchange
with the living God;
we must be willing to give up the ineffectual,
if comfortable,
homage to an idol who demands nothing,
in favor of the challenging God of Christ who
offers abundant life—or nothing.

As great as is the urge to
misname the problem so it does not touch us
is the thought,
"Those are big problems,
I am a little person;
there is nothing I can do."
But where do John McCaffrey and Louis Epstein
live?
The loneliness, emptiness, frustration
of their lives are at your door.
Perhaps it is your loneliness, emptiness and
    frustration.
It certainly might not be
for you
a matter of carrying posters, protesting in
    rallies
or becoming a Mother Teresa.
But it *is* a matter
of at least smiling at your fellow
parishioner at church next Sunday;
it is a matter of grasping and giving a
friendly handshake at Mass—
at least that.
If Calcutta is far away,
the doors of your parish center are not.

In reality, is it not
always
a matter of "curing" one person at a time
and, in that curing, becoming more whole
    yourself?

If only the stories were told,
the stories of those about you!
It is important that someone cares enough
to see and to ask.
Care enough to listen and, in
listening,
become the very ears of God.

I have said such exchanging
is important.
I have no right to do that.
Each of us must decide for ourselves
if it is important or not.
Each of us must decide who
our God will be.

Vatican II declared over
ten years ago
that the Church is not our buildings;
the Church is a community of believers.
It is a faithed community laying claim to a
        single
vision, a single power, to a common God.
We are to be a people who have shared an
        experience—
the death and resurrection of our Lord—
through whom and in whom
we have begun to pass to our own life out of
our own death.
From that common experience comes our
        strength
and our cohesion,
from this Christ-encounter come our
priorities and our reason for being.

PRIORITIES

But
are our churches people?
Are our people bound together
by a common faith, a common experience?
Do we even profess the same God
beneath our routinely recited Nicene Creed?
Have we seriously asked the
fundamental questions:
God who? For what? How?
Is there the kind of
"life" happening within our living Churches
that would give evidence of the exchange
all holiness demands?

Could we detect, clearly, that
Holy Communion means for our people
"holy" because it is the essence of
God's exchange with us;
that Holy Mass is
"holy" because it is the ritual within which
we proclaim and deepen the exchange
that alone makes holy to be holy;
that our holy water and holy days and
Holy Mother Church mean *exchange*,
mean trading our slavery and blindness
for God's gift of light and freedom?
And if they don't, then what are we doing
in those buildings week after week?
God gives us love,
authentic, free, genuine love.
Is that love being given?

God is freedom for men.
We claim we desire a free society
but slaves cannot birth freedom while in
slavery;
we cannot give what is not
within us.

Ruth,
let us call her that,
just came to see me.
She has three children and is separated from
a drinking alcoholic husband.
She and all connected to this family
live in a sea of misery and hatred.
All are unnamed slaves.
Ruth, even as she came in the door,
was high on her very legal, very prescribed
nerve pills.
Several years ago Ruth attempted suicide
with gin and sleeping tablets.
She may try again.

She curses God because he
won't help her.
She doesn't want God; she wants God
in the form of a pill she can take
to make all things okay again
(and they never were okay).
She wants God to "do his thing"
so she won't have to do anything for herself.
She is sick and tired but
not sick and tired enough to reach out for all
    the help
that is available.
And it is available.
She has not hurt enough to be pushed to
desperation,
to the point of letting go.

She will make changes
in her life but not allow
change to take place.
We can handle changes
without desperation—they are
variations of the same thing.
But we seldom get around to
change—
trying something new—
without desperation.
Many people never find God until they
kiss concrete,
whatever that concrete happens to be
in their personal lives.
When we are confronted by
". . . that point beyond which we cannot go
    alone,"
then are we forced to die
or surrender to God.

Ruth did verbalize a burning truth
as she half-stared out the empty window:
"I am so lonely I could die."
And she may.

Who will talk to Ruth?
Even if she wanted to trust, how many
are there to take her seriously enough
to offer her truth to feed on,
strength to stand on her own feet,
love enough to surrender to the Covenant
        God?
Who can see her there,
straddling the chute as the dense coal dust
settles around her?
Mr. Fox couldn't see John
Can we see Ruth?

Ruth is a regular churchgoer.
That is, she regularly goes to a building
with a saint's name painted on it.
The last thing in her mind is that
"church"
has anything to do with serenity, exchange or
        growth.
It is a place where God can find her,
not where she can find God.
In her self-hatred she cannot accept
that anyone loves her,
that anyone cares.
But that is why we have community,
". . . so we know what is going on in heaven."

Ruth and John and Louis
are with us now.
Perhaps they are us.
If any real change is to happen, it will be due
to finding our God
and destroying an idol.

There is nothing more important
taking place on this planet of men
than the process of spiritual liberation
which,
in its fullness, means finding the
God who is love.

But we must decide.
What will be is what
we cause to be,
what we allow to be.
So be it.